Assessment Supplement

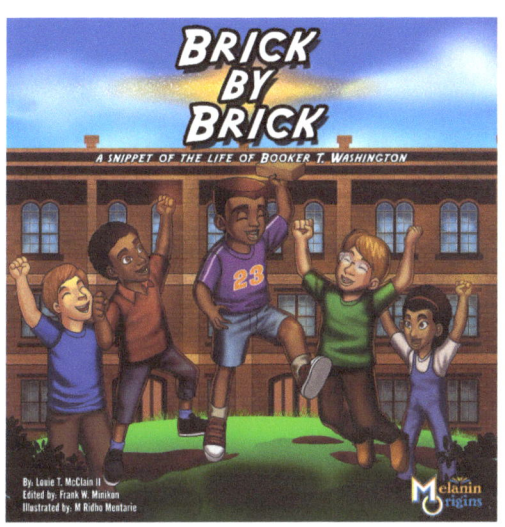

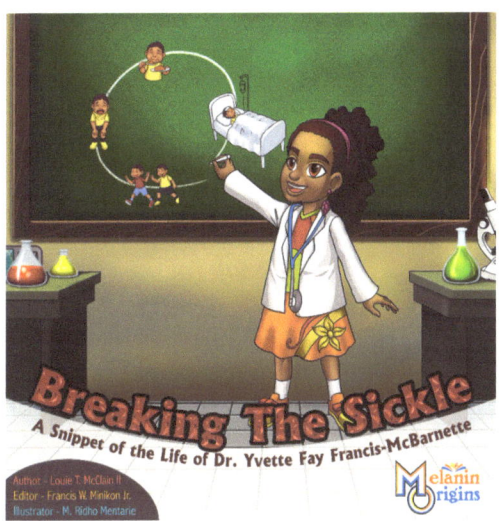

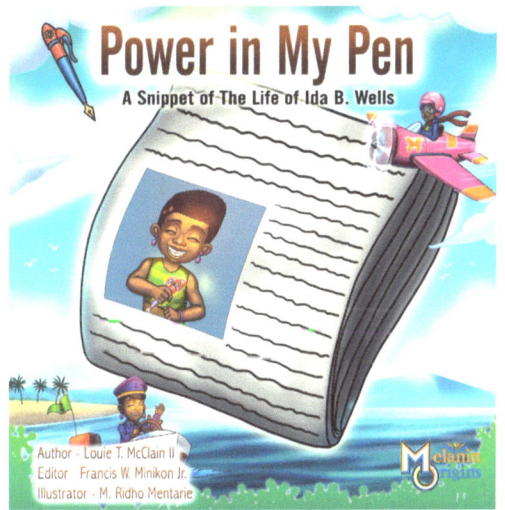

Grade 1

Created by The Cole Lab LLC
Your Development Destination

OUR MISSION

To provide quality educational materials which inspire young minds to aspire for excellence while embracing their heritage.

OUR VISION

To become the largest Culturally Competent book provider in the United States of America.

OUR CORE VALUES

EDUCATIONAL EMPOWERMENT

Sparking an interest in books and encouraging reading at a young age.

PROMOTING STRONG FAMILIES

Reviving the parent / child relationship through family readings, dialogue, discussion and debate.

CULTURAL CONFIDENCE

Instilling a pure, strong, healthy knowledge of self at a young age.

©The Cole Lab LLC 2017
©Melanin Origins LLC 2017

A Note:

Melanin Origins LLC is committed to literacy and empowerment through powerful images and stories representative of diverse backgrounds and cultural pride. Our books are the perfect addition to any primary classroom for the benefit of all students.

This document is a TEKS focused assessment supplement which allows for seamless implementation of Melanin Origins LLC learning materials with the grade 1 reader. The TEKS/STAAR objectives assessed herein are:

Readiness Standards Grade One Reading & Grade One Writing:
1.1(F) identify information that different parts of a book provide

1.2(A) decode words in context and isolation by applying common letter-sound correspondences

1.4 (B) ask relevant questions, seek clarification, and locate facts and details about stories and other texts

1.6 (A) identify words that name actions (verbs) and words that name persons, places, or things (nouns)

1.9 (B) describe characters in a story and the reasons for their actions and feelings

1.10 Literary Non-fiction Students understand, make inferences and draw conclusions about the varied structural patterns and features of literary nonfiction and respond by providing evidence from text to support their understanding

Fig.19(E) retell or act out important events in stories in logical order

Fig. 19(F) make connections to own experiences, to ideas in other texts, and to the larger community and discuss textual evidence

TABLE OF CONTENTS

Brick By Brick Assessment One............................... 5

Brick By Brick Assessment Two.............................. 6

Breaking the Sickle Assessment One..................... 8

Breaking the Sickle Assessment Two..................... 9

Power in My Pen Assessment One...................... 11

Power in My Pen Assessment Two...................... 12

Words Assessment ………………………………….. 14

Matching & Additional Questions …………………. 15

Answer Key ………………………………………….. 16

Brick By Brick
A Snippet of the Life of Booker T. Washington

Assessment One
(accessing background knowledge)

1. Booker T. Washington is…

   a. A famous football player   c. A famous educator
   b. A famous actor   d. A famous banker

2. True or False You can get things done by doing one step at a time.

3. When we are with our friends having fun, we feel…
   a. Sad
   b. Angry
   c. Excited

4. The Tuskegee farmers grew…
   a. Fruits and vegetables
   b. Coffee
   c. Flowers
   d. Bushes

5. Circle the items that do not belong in each column:

a. Bananas	a. Corn
b. Grapes	b. Apples
c. Peaches	c. Peas
d. Green Beans	d. Broccoli

6. People like Booker T. Washington because he was…
   a. A bully   c. A fighter
   b. A comedian   d. A leader

Brick By Brick
A Snippet of the Life of Booker T. Washington
Assessment Two

1. True or False Booker T. Washington did everything by himself.

2. Booker T. Washington built...

    a. The Tuskegee Institute
    b. The White House
    c. The Statue of Liberty
    d. The Great Wall of China

3. Who helped him?

    a. His family
    b. His friends
    c. Other doctors
    d. Strangers

4. In this picture, how are the characters feeling? Circle One:
    a. Sad
    b. Angry
    c. Excited

5. Why do people like him? Circle One

    a. He is artistic.
    b. He is funny.
    c. He is a leader.
    d. He is a bully.

6. What does Booker T. Washington like to do? Select all that apply

a. Talk in front of large crowds
b. Play football
c. Ride horses
d. Teach students who visit him in class

7. What important person sometimes asks to speak with Booker T. Washington?

   a. The president
   b. The principal
   c. Scientists
   d. His mother

8. At the Tuskegee Institute, what did he and his friends grow?

   a. Phones and ipads
   b. Leaves and vines
   c. Fruits and vegetables
   d. Beans and flowers

9. Circle the item that does not belong in each column:

   a. Carrots
   b. Peas
   c. Apples
   d. Green Beans

   a. Grapes
   b. Lettuce
   c. Oranges
   d. Lemons

10. Which two words almost mean the same thing?

    a.   Create   Build
    b.   Farm   City
    c.   Help   Hurt
    d.   Work   Play

Breaking the Sickle
A Snippet of the Life of Dr. Yvette Fay Francis-McBarnette

Assessment One
(accessing background knowledge)

1. You demonstrate true love and friendship by:
   a. Making money
   b. Helping those you care most about
   c. Eating Candy
   d. FIghting with friends

2. The word "cycle" reminds us of what shape?
   a. Square
   b. Triangle
   c. Circle
   d. Rectangle

3. Sickle Cell is a disease that effects your:
   a. Feet
   b. Hair
   c. Ears
   d. Blood

4. All of these are ways to honor your parents except:
   a. Making good grades in school
   b. Reading books
   c. Doing your chores
   d. Talking back

5. A person with Sickle Cell Disease will...
   a. Be full of energy
   b. Have a hard time breathing
   c. Have no pain
   d. Forget lots of stuff

6. True or False People should focus on having as much fun as they can and not worry about working hard.

Breaking the Sickle
A Snippet of the Life of Dr. Yvette Fay Francis-McBarnette
Assessment Two

1. Yvette learned at a young age that true love and friendship are demonstrated by:

    a. Making money
    b. Eating candy
    c. Playing with friends
    d. Helping the ones you care most about

2. The word "Cycle" reminds us of what shape?

    a. Rectangle
    b. Circle
    c. Square
    d. Triangle

3. Sickle Cell is a disease that effects your _____.

    a. Blood
    b. Feet
    c. Hair
    d. Ears

4. When did Dr. Yvette leave Jamaica?

    a. When she was a teenager
    b. When she was a grown-up
    c. When she was a baby
    d. When she was an old lady

5. Yvette honored her mother and father by doing all of the following except?

    a. Reading books
    b. Doing chores
    c. Talking back
    d. Making good grades in school

6. After high school, Yvette went to
   _____.

   a. The store
   b. Her friend's house
   c. College
   d. The park

7. A person with Sickle Cell disease will feel all of the following except…

   a. You will forget a lot of things
   b. You will have great pain in your body
   c. You will be tired
   d. You will have a hard time breathing

8. Yvette worked in a…

   a. House
   b. Hospital
   c. Backyard
   d. Bank

9. True or False Yvette got to meet the president of the United States of America.

10. True or False   Yvette says everyone should focus on fun instead of work.

Power in My Pen
A Snippet of the Life of Ida B. Wells

Assessment One
(accessing background knowledge)

1. *Power in My Pen* is mostly about...

    a. Growing up
    b. Writing
    c. Drawing pictures
    d. Making pretty clothes

2. True or False Ida B. Wells was famous for her songs.

3. Editing means...

    a. Adding pictures
    b. Sharing with others
    c. Making a book
    d. Making sure everything comes out right

4. It is fun to read stories that are?

    a. Boring
    b. Exciting
    c. Confusing
    d. Both B & C

5. True or False It is important to always tell the truth.

6. When someone is doing what they love, how does it make them feel?

    a. Angry
    b. Frustrated
    c. Sad
    d. Happy

Power in My Pen
A Snippet of the Life of Ida B. Wells
Assessment Two

1. Ida B. Wells says, "when paper and pen come together, the world will know that I am _____."

    a. Happy
    b. Clever
    c. Sad
    d. Busy

2. This story is mostly about
    a. Family
    b. Building
    c. Growing
    d. Writing

3. How many brothers and sisters did Ida B. Wells have?
    a. 3
    b. 4
    c. 5
    d. 6

4. Ida B. Wells really liked to…
    a. Play the trombone
    b. Draw pictures
    c. Eat candy
    d. Teach students

5. Ida B. Wells used to write stories for…
    a. Library books
    b. School books
    c. Competitions
    d. The local newspaper

© Melanin Origins LLC 2018 © The Cole Lab LLC 2018

6. Editing means
    a. Adding pictures
    b. Making sure everything comes out right
    c. Sharing with others
    d. Making a book

7. What is the secret to Ida's power in her pen?
    a. Telling the truth
    b. Being creative
    c. Adding lots of details
    d. Making it pretty

8. What is the opposite of truth?
    a. Funny
    b. Interesting
    c. Create
    d. Lie

9. True or False Ida B. Wells never listened to her Granny.

10. When Ida is writing, she is …

    a. Angry
    b. Hungry
    c. Happy
    d. Sad

Words

1. How many syllables are in the word <u>together</u>?
   a. 1 b. 2 c. 3

2. How many syllables are in the word <u>broken</u>?
   a. 1
   b. 2
   c. 3

3. How many word parts are in the word <u>cared</u>?
   a. 1
   b. 2
   c. 3

4. How many word parts are in the word <u>shortly</u>?
   a. 1
   b. 2
   c. 3

5. Granny means
   a. Father
   b. Mother
   c. God mother
   d. Grandmother

6. The word <u>can't</u> means
   a. Cans
   b. Do it
   c. Can not
   d. Do not

7. The word raised comes from the word
   a. Risk
   b. Raise
   c. Rinse
   d. Ray

8. A word that means the opposite of <u>love</u> is
   a. Laugh
   b. Play
   c. Hate
   d. Sad

9. <u>Playing</u> is a
   a. Verb (action)
   b. Noun (person)
   c. Noun (place)
   d. Noun (thing)

10. <u>School</u> is a
    a. Verb (action)
    b. Noun (person)
    c. Noun (place)
    d. Noun (thing)

Additional Questions

1. These books are what kind of passage?
   a. Poems
   b. Stories
   c. Letters
   d. News Articles

2. All of the characters focused on…
   a. Making money
   b. Helping others
   c. Traveling
   d. Having fun

Matching Section

Match the character with the book.

_____ Ida B. Wells   *a. Brick By Brick*
_____ Booker T. Washington   *b. Breaking the Sickle*
_____ Yvette F. Francis-McBarnette   *c. Power in My Pen*

Match the character with their title.

_____ Ida B. Wells   a. Medical doctor
_____ Booker T. Washington   b. Journalist
_____ Yvette F. Francis-McBarnette   c. Educator

Answer Key

One Assessment *Brick By Brick*
1. c
2. true
3. c
4. a
5. d, b
6. d

Assessment One *Breaking the Sickle*
1. b
2. c
3. d
4. d
5. b
6. false

One Assessment *Power in My Pen*
1. b
2. false
3. d
4. b
5. true
6. d

Brick By Brick Assessment Two
1. false
2. a
3. a
4. c
5. c
6. a, d
7. a
8. c
9. c, b
10. a

Breaking the Sickle Assessment Two
1. d
2. b
3. a
4. c
5. c
6. c
7. a
8. b
9. true
10. false

Power in My Pen Assessment Two
1. b
2. d
3. c
4. d
5. d
6. b
7. a
8. d
9. false
10. c

Words
1. c
2. b
3. b
4. b
5. d
6. c
7. b
8. c
9. a
10. c

Additional Questions
1. b
2. b

Matching
1. c, a, b
2. b, c, a

Melanin Origins LLC is committed to providing quality books and supplemental materials for all students. For more titles and resources, please, visit our website at

www.melaninorigins.com.

©The Cole Lab LLC 2017
©Melanin Origins LLC 2017

 Assessment Supplement

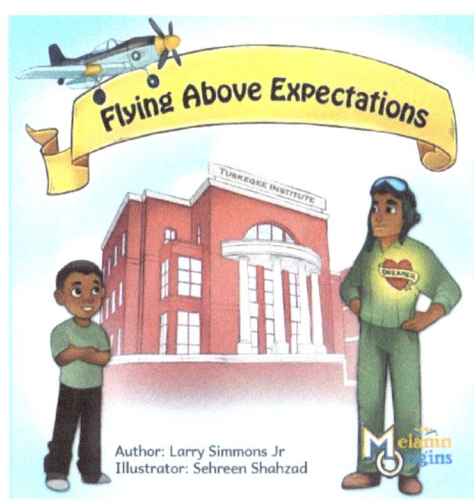

Grade 1

Created by The Cole Lab LLC
Your Development Destination

© Melanin Origins LLC 2018 © The Cole Lab LLC 2018

Table of Contents

Flying Above Expectations Assessment One 21

Flying Above Expectations Assessment Two 22

Louisiana Belle Assessment One 24

Louisiana Belle Assessment Two 25

Education is Power Assessment One 27

Education is Power Assessment Two 28

Additional Questions 30

Matching Section 30

Answer Key 31

Flying Above Expectations

Assessment One
(accessing background knowledge)

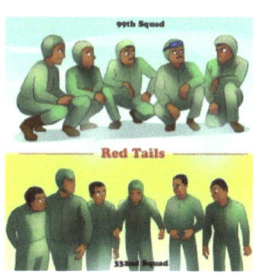

1. Write at least 2 sentences telling what you want to be when you grow up and why.

   _____

   _____

2. When people tell you that it is impossible to be what you want to be, what should you do?
   a. believe them and give up
   b. cry
   C. hit them
   D. try even harder and do what it takes to make your dreams come true

3. Circle **True** or **False** Teachers are the only adults who can teach you how to work hard.

4. When someone accomplishes their dreams, they feel _____.
   A. Proud
   B. Disappointed
   C. Scared
   D. Silly

5. Anything is _____ if you believe.
   A. Impossible
   B. Possible
   C. Nice

6. A pilot is a person who _____
   A. Drives a cab
   B. Flies an airplane
   C. Bakes pies

Flying Above Expectations
Assessment Two

1. The author wrote this text to ___.
   A. Persuade us to fly airplanes
   B. Tell us to never give up on our dreams just like Chief Anderson never gave up on his
   C. Explain the steps to being a part of the Tuskegee Airmen

2. Anderson's dad was a great influence on his life because he ___.
   A. Taught him the importance of hard work
   B. Bought him toys
   C. Talked to him

3. What event belongs in the empty box?

   | Anderson thinks about buying an airplane | → | ? | → | Anderson buys an airplane. |

   A. Anderson's dad teaches him the value of hard work
   B. Anderson learns how to fly an airplane
   C. Anderson served in the military and showed hard work and discipline

4. When people made fun of Anderson and told him no, he probably felt ___.
   A. Excited
   B. Upset
   C. Happy

5. Write about a time someone made fun of you.

   _____
   _____

© Melanin Origins LLC 2018 © The Cole Lab LLC 2018

6. What happened to make Chief Anderson feel confident about getting his pilot's license?
   A. His dad told him the value of hard work
   B. People told him that he couldn't be a pilot
   C. He practiced flying by taking his friends places

7. Why did the author title this book "Flying Above Expectations"?
   A. He wants kids to learn to fly airplanes
   B. He wants kids to see that they can rise above what others expect of them and accomplish great things like Chief Anderson did
   C. He wants to show the reader how the Tuskegee Airmen flew airplanes

8. Circle the word that makes a long vowel sound.
   A. Expectations
   B. Fly
   C. Chief
   D. Work

9. Chief Anderson didn't give up flying after he crashed his airplane because _____.
   A. He needed to earn money.
   B. He had a passion for flying and wanted to accomplish his dream of being a pilot
   C. His dad would be upset with him

10. Which words help you understand the meaning of pilot in this text?
    A. Learn how to fly
    B. Did well in school
    C. Bought his own plane

11. After reading this text, the reader can conclude that Chief Anderson ---
    A. Enjoyed his years in school
    B. Overcame obstacles not just for himself but to help others
    C. Was disappointed that no one would teach him how to fly

Louisiana Belle
A Snippet of the Life of Madam CJ Walker

Assessment One
(accessing background knowledge)

1. What would you do with a million dollars?
   _____
   _____
   _____

2. Who are people who invent things that make the world or life in the world better?
   A. Writer
   B. Inventor
   C. Creator

3. Circle the item that is **NOT** natural.
   A. Rocks
   B. Dirt
   C. Statue of Liberty

4. Circle **True or False**. Hard work always pays off.

5. What does being successful mean to you?
   _____
   _____

6. Which example is **NOT** a way to help others?
   A. Give money to the homeless
   B. Help students go to college by giving them scholarships
   C. Ignore a new student who asks you a question

© Melanin Origins LLC 2018 © The Cole Lab LLC 2018

Louisiana Belle
A Snippet of the Life of Madam C.J. Walker
Assessment Two

1. What was something people thought Madam C.J. Walker invented that she really didn't?
   A. Perm	B. Shampoo	C. Pomades

2. Circle **True or False**. Madam C.J. Walker wanted to help people, so she could be rich.

3. Which paragraph is the best way to retell this story?
   A. Madam C.J. Walker wanted to be rich, so she decided to make hair products for women and then became a millionaire.
   B. Madam C.J. Walker wanted to help others, so she created hair products for women with natural hair to look as fabulous as she did. People loved her products, and that made her a lot of money. She, then, decided to give back to others with her money.
   C. Madam C.J. Walker became a millionaire and then helped others by creating hair products to help them have beautiful hair like hers.

4. The author most likely wrote this text to---
   A. Show the reader that money is important to live a good life
   B. Tell the reader that you can do awesome things, and you should help others when you become successful
   C. Persuade the reader to have natural hair because it's beautiful

5. Why did Madam C.J. Walker say "money is not everything?"
   A. Because money is not important to her
   B. Because having too much money makes you a bad person
   C. Because money shouldn't be the most important thing to make you happy, but it is good to use to help others

6. When Madam C.J. Walker says she is a self-made millionaire, she means
   A. She made up the word millionaire.

B. She made herself a millionaire by what she did to help others.
C. She was from Louisiana.

7. The illustrator probably made pictures of Madam C.J. Walker helping people in order to—
   A. Show the reader how she used her money to make life better for others
   B. Make the reader think she is cool
   C. Show the reader what they should do when they get money

8. How did Madam C.J. Walker make money?
   A. Making clothes
   B. Writing books
   C. Creating hair products to help women

9. Which event could NOT fit in this box?

   | Madam CJ Walker went out of her way to give money to people who needed help the most. | ➡ | ? |

   A. Madam C.J. Walker gives money to clubs to help the community
   B. Madam C.J. Walker creates hair products for women to have fabulous hair
   C. Madam C.J. Walker gives money to Booker for his school in Tuskegee

10. What does the word fabulous mean in this text?
    A. Beautiful   B. Ugly   C. Important

11. What is one thing Madam CJ Walker did NOT do in this text in order to help other people?
    A. Give money to students for scholarships, so they could go to school
    B. Give money to her friend to help his school in Tuskegee
    C. Give money to animal shelters, so stray dogs can have better homes

12. What is something you want to invent to help others, and how will it help them?
    _____
    _____

Education Is Power
Snippet of the Life of W.E.B. Du Bois

Assessment One
(accessing background knowledge)

1. Circle **True or False**. Getting an education won't help me in life.

2. Write about why you come to school.

   _____

   _____

   _____

3. Without an education, it will be difficult for me to be _____.
    a. Fun
    b. Gorgeous
    c. Successful

4. If I want to be whatever I want to when I grow up, I need to _____.
    a. Stay in school and do my best
    b. Stay at home from school
    c. Come to school late

5. Knowledge is _____.
    a. Power
    b. Nice
    c. A waste of time

6. Why is your teacher important to you?

   _____

   _____

Education Is Power
A Snippet of the Life of W.E.B. Du Bois
Assessment Two

1. Which of these is **NOT** a reason why W. E. B. Du Bois thinks education is power?
   A. Helps you to be a great learner and teacher
   B. Gives you a better understanding of the world
   C. Gives you a job where you can make a lot of money

2. W. E. B. Du Bois's teacher was important to him because—
   A. She inspired him to use his education to be who he wanted to be
   B. She gave him extra recess
   C. She gave him A's on his report card

3. We can conclude that W. E. B. Du Bois valued his education because—
   A. He continued to share education wherever he went
   B. He loved learning so much that he went to college 3 times
   C. Both A and B

4. When W. E. B. Du Bois said there is no limit, no limit means—
   A. Everything is Impossible
   B. Anything is Possible
   C. He could spend what he wanted

5. According to the text, after attending Harvard, W. E. B. ____
   A. Got married
   B. Created a group known as the Talented Tenth and helped start the NAACP
   C. Attended the University of Berlin in Germany

6. Circle **True or False**   Education can take you all around the world.

7. What was W. E. B. Du Bois's favorite part about being in a country far from home?
    A. The food was delicious!
    B. Learning things about the cultures and ways of living that were different from America
    C. Getting an education

8. Using your brainpower gives you the ability to be whoever you want to be, go wherever you want to go, and _____.
    A. Do whatever you want to do
    B. Play whenever you want to play
    C. Say whatever you want to say

9. The author most likely wrote this text to—
    A. Encourage you to get an education
    B. Persuade you to travel to a different country
    C. Give you tips on how to survive life in college

10. The title of this text gives us a clue about—
    A. One of W. E. B. Du Bois' beliefs
    B. The meaning of education
    C. What his mom told him in the book

Additional Questions

1. Which two people can we conclude were good friends?
   A. Booker T. Washington and Madam C.J. Walker
   B. Booker T. Washington and W.E.B. DuBois
   C. Chief Anderson and Madam C.J. Walker

2. Who most likely did NOT know Booker T. Washington personally?
   A. Chief Anderson
   B. Madam C.J. Walker
   C. W.E.B. DuBois

3. Which of these African Americans was NOT discussed in these books?
   A. W.E.B. DuBois
   B. Madam C.J. Walker
   C. Dr. Martin Luther King Jr.

Matching Section

1. Match the character with the book.

   _____ W.E.B. Dubois   A. Flying Above Expectations
   _____ Madame C. J. Walker   B. Education is Power
   _____ Chief Anderson   C. Louisiana Belle

2. Match the character with the title.

   _____ W.E.B. DuBois   A. Educator
   _____ Madame C.J. Walker   B. Pilot
   _____ Chief Anderson   C. Inventor

Answer Key

Flying Above Expectations Assessment One
1. Answers may vary but should be logical.
2. D
3. False
4. A
5. B
6. B

Flying Above Expectations Assessment Two
1. B
2. A
3. C
4. B
5. Answers may vary but should be a logical response.
6. C
7. B
8. B
9. A
10. B

Louisiana Belle Assessment One
1. Answers may vary but should logically answer the question.
2. B
3. C
4. True
5. Answers may vary but should logically answer the question according to the meaning of the word successful.
6. C

Louisiana Belle Assessment Two
1. a
2. False
3. B
4. B
5. C
6. B
7. A
8. C

9. B
10. A
11. C
12. Answers may vary but should logically answer the questions.

Education is Power Assessment One
1. False
2. Answers may vary
3. C
4. A
5. A
6. Answers may vary

Education is Power Assessment Two
1. C
2. A
3. C
4. B
5. B
6. True
7. B
8. A
9. A
10. A

Other Questions
1. A
2. C
3. C

Matching
1. B, C, A
2. A, C, B

Melanin Origins LLC is committed to providing quality books and supplemental materials for all students. For more titles and resources, please, visit our website at

www.melaninorigins.com.

www.ingramcontent.com/pod-product-compliance
Lightning Source LLC
Chambersburg PA
CBHW041602070526
44586CB00003BA/56